Poptropica® English

WORKBOOK 6

T0352589

Future Island

José Luis Morales • John Wiltshier • Aaron Jolly
Series Advisor: David Nunan

Pearson Education Limited
Edinburgh Gate
Harlow
Essex CM20 2JE
England
and Associated Companies throughout the world.

Poptropica English

© Pearson Education Limited 2015

Based on the work of Aaron Jolly

The rights of John Wiltshire, José Luis Morales, and Aaron Jolly to be identified as authors of this work have been asserted by them in accordance with the Copyright, Designs and Patents Act 1988.

Phonics syllabus and activities by Rachel Wilson

Editorial, design, and project management by hyphen

First published 2015

Tenth impression 2022

ISBN: 978-1-292-11249-7

Set in Fiendstar 13/20pt

Printed in Slovakia by Neografia

The publisher would like to thank the following for their kind permission to reproduce their photographs:

(Key: b-bottom; c-center, l-left; r-right; t-top)

123RF.com: flaperval 35l, gavran333 71cl, get4net 44b, Margie Hurwich 64, kessudap 71r, Paul Maguire 71tr, pr2is 21l, Tom Tietz 25t, Maksym Topchii 16l; **Alamy Images:** Oliver Gerhard 24, Andrew Roland 35r, Zoonar Gmbh 35c; **Digital Vision:** 25b; **Fotolia.com:** creativenature. nl 71l, EcoView 21cl, Wong Sze Fei 61, Sabphoto 34l; **Getty Images:** Stockbyte 84; **Jupiterimages:** 26cl; **Pearson Education Ltd:** MindStudio 11, Miguel Domínguez Muñoz 16cl; **Shutterstock.com:** Paul Banton 26r, Sanjay Deva 44c, DnDavis 16r, East 34r, Four Oaks 26cr, Jan Kratochvila 26l, Photobank.ch 44t, Stuart G Porter 21r, Rohit Seth 16cr, Martin Valigursky 21cr, Tracy Whiteside 54, Oleg Znamenskiy 21c

Illustrators: Illias Arahovitis (Beehive Illustration), Leo Cultura, Mark Draisey, Michael Garton (The Bright Agency), John Haslam, Ned Jolliffe (Eye Candy Illustration), Moira Millman, Ken Mok, Zaharias Papadopoulos (hyphen) Rui Ricardo (Folio Art), Christos Skaltsas (hyphen) and Olimpia Wong

All other images © Pearson Education Limited

Every effort has been made to trace the copyright holders and we apologize in advance for any unintentional omissions. We would be pleased to insert the appropriate acknowledgement in any subsequent edition of this publication.

Contents

Welcome

1 Check (✓).

1 Who uses the THD?

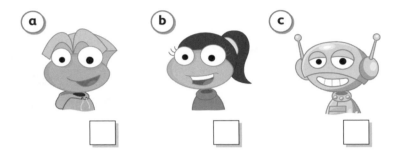

a   b   c

☐   ☐   ☐

2 Who says she wants to go home?

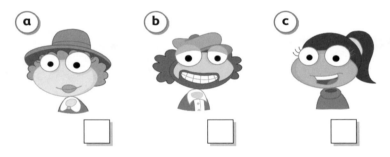

a   b   c

☐   ☐   ☐

2 Circle T = True or F = False.

1 Matt knows the man and the woman who are in his office.   T / F

2 Matt is tired because it's late at night.   T / F

3 The mysterious woman doesn't want to leave.   T / F

4 The THD is working very well.   T / F

5 Matt and AL time-travel to 1950.   T / F

6 Bella understands the problem with the THD.   T / F

3 Write the names of the characters.

AL   Bella   Matt   The mysterious couple

1

2

3

4

_____   _____   _____   _____

4 Look at Activity 3 and number.

a   He is Matt's droid assistant. He was made with expensive technology.
He helps Matt solve difficult problems.

b   They came to Science Park to find a time-travel machine. They took
the THD. Now they want to go home. They are smart and fast.

c   He is a time engineer. He works in a very modern office. He is
hard-working and patient. He often works until late at night.

d   She joins Matt and AL on their mission. She will try to help them find
the mysterious couple. She is smart, creative, and helpful.

5 Circle. What do you think will happen in the story?

1   Matt, AL, and Bella will (help / catch) the mysterious couple.

2   Bella (will / will not) stay with Matt and AL until the end of the story.

3   They will (time-travel / go by flying car) to many amazing places.

4   The mysterious couple (will / will not) return to their home happily.

6 Match.

1	1st	**a**	forty-second
2	7th	**b**	thirteenth
3	13th	**c**	ninety-ninth
4	20th	**d**	seventh
5	28th	**e**	sixty-fifth
6	42nd	**f**	twentieth
7	65th	**g**	first
8	99th	**h**	twenty-eighth

7 **Listen and circle.**

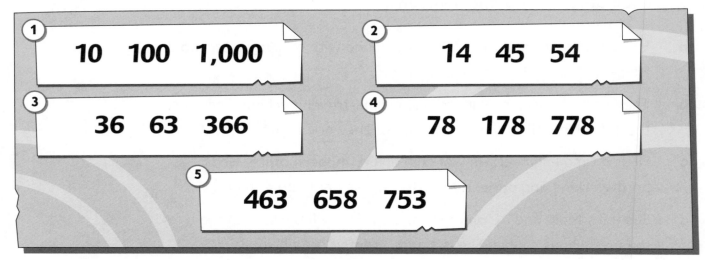

1 10   100   1,000

2 14   45   54

3 36   63   366

4 78   178   778

5 463   658   753

8 Write.

1 first, second, third, _____

2 fifteenth, sixteenth, _____, eighteenth

3 twentieth, _____, fortieth, fiftieth

4 eleventh, twenty-first, thirty-first, _____

5 sixty-sixth, sixty-seventh, _____, sixty-ninth

6 _____, ninety-eighth, ninety-seventh, ninety-sixth

9 Write.

cold   furry   hard   loud   spiky   sweet

1 The ice is _____.   **2** The chocolate is _____.

3 The music is _____.   **4** The hair is _____.

5 The spider is _____.   **6** The rock is _____.

10 Think and write.

1 <u>Shells are</u> _____ smooth.

2 _____ round.

3 _____ soft.

4 _____ scary.

5 _____ cute.

6 _____ loud.

11 🎧 **03** Listen and check (✓). Then write.

chocolate   a fish   a rose   a stuffed lion

	looks	feels	smells	sounds	tastes	What is it?
1	wet ☐ scary ☐	rough ☐ cold ☐	like the ocean ☐ like a lemon ☐			_____
2		soft ☐ hard ☐		scary ☐ nice ☐		_____
3	brown ☐ black ☐	smooth ☐ sharp ☐	great ☐ bad ☐		sour ☐ sweet ☐	_____
4	beautiful ☐ bad ☐	furry ☐ spiky ☐	sweet ☐ good ☐			_____

⭐ **Are you ready for Unit 1?**

1 Adventure camp

1 Write the names of the characters.

Felipe   Flo   Hannah   Maria   Tom

 1 _____

 2 _____

 3 _____

 4 _____

 5 _____

2 Unscramble and write. Then number.

1 ttne   _____

2 ria mupp   _____

3 geps   _____

4 thaflishgl   _____

5 srift-dia itk _____

6 isleengp gba _____

7 rai sestarmt _____

8 pomcssa   _____

9 slepo   _____

a 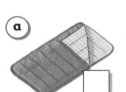 ☐

b ☐

c  ☐

d  ☐

e ☐

f  ☐

g  ☐

h  ☐

i  ☐

3 Look at Flo's list. Listen and ✓ or ✗.

List for adventure camp

a backpack   ☐   an air mattress ☐   an mp3 player   ☐

a flashlight ☐   an air pump   ☐   a sleeping bag ☐

pegs   ☐   books   ☐   a first-aid kit ☐

a compass   ☐

4 **Circle.**

1 I like (play / playing) soccer, but I (don't / doesn't) like camping.

2 He doesn't like (watch / watching) TV. He (like / likes) reading.

3 They're (Brazil / British). They're (live / from) the United Kingdom.

4 We're good (at dancing / dancing). We (never / always) practice.

5 She loves jumping on the trampoline and (ski / skiing). She thinks they're (fun / boring).

6 He's good (at singing / at sing). He's a famous (soldier / musician).

5 **Listen and circle.**

1 Tom has one (sister / brother).

2 Maria likes dancing, but she's not good at (singing / swimming).

3 Flo is from the (United States / United Kingdom). She's good at (skiing / swimming), and she loves talking to friends.

4 Felipe likes science and (English / math).

6 **Draw yourself. Then write.**

My name's _____.

I'm from _____

in _____.

I love _____

and _____,

but I don't like _____.

I'm good at _____

and _____,

but I'm not good at _____.

7 **Number.**

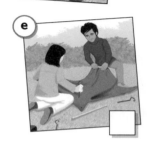

1 They're lighting a fire.

2 He's setting up the bed.

3 They're covering their heads.

4 He's putting in the pegs.

5 She's reading a compass.

6 They're taking down the tent

7 It's keeping out the rain.

8 They're pitching the tent.

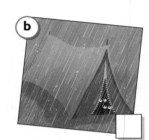

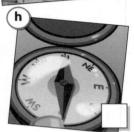

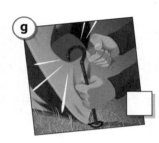

8 **Write.**

1 The dog <u>is running</u> _____.

2 The two boys _____.

3 The girl _____.

4 The man _____.

5 The two girls _____.

9 **Listen and circle.**

1 I (can / can't) read a book, but I (can / can't) read a map.

2 They (can / can't) swim, but they (can / can't) pitch a tent.

3 They (can / can't) put in the pegs, (and / but) they can light a fire.

4 She likes reading comic books, (and / but) she (can / can't) read a compass.

5 We can pitch a tent, (and / but) we (can / can't) take down a tent, too.

10 **Listen and write what Sandy can and can't do.**

Can
1 She can _____.
2 _____
_____
3 _____
_____
4 _____
_____

Can't
1 She can't _____.
2 _____
_____
3 _____
_____
4 _____
_____

11 **What can you do?**

What can you do?
1 _____
2 _____
3 _____
4 _____

What can't you do?
1 _____
2 _____
3 _____
4 _____

12 Check (✓).

1   Who knows where the mysterious couple are going?

2   Who is very good at computers?

13 Correct the sentences.

1   Bella doesn't like camping.

_____

2   Matt says Bella can't come with them.

_____

3   They're going to Asia.

_____

14 Write. Then number the story events in order.

> Africa   Bella   camp   girl   THD   time-travel

☐ They meet a _____ named Bella.

☐ Matt says that _____ can come with them.

☐ They follow the mysterious couple to _____.

☐ Matt and AL time-travel to an adventure _____.

☐ Bella wants to _____ with Matt and AL.

☐ Bella makes the _____ work again.

15 Match.

Situation

1 When you get into a car

2 In rocky places on the coast

3 At home

4 In a swimming pool

5 In windy, stormy weather

6 During take-off and landing on a plane

VALUES

Safety first. Think about safety when you go camping.

f Don't stand under trees!

e Don't use electrical things near water!

d Don't dive or swim!

The safe thing to do

a Fasten your seatbelt!

b Look before you dive!

c Buckle up!

16 Look and ✗ the activities you don't want to try.

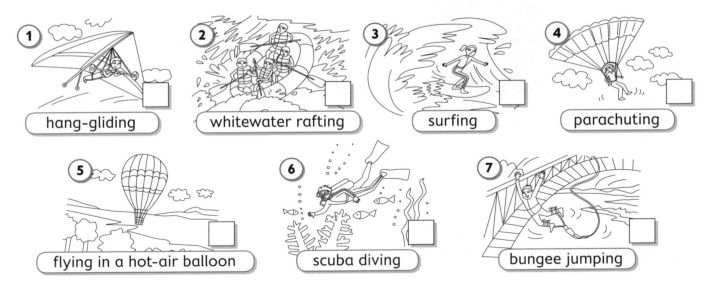

1 hang-gliding

2 whitewater rafting

3 surfing

4 parachuting

5 flying in a hot-air balloon

6 scuba diving

7 bungee jumping

Hello Grandpa,

How are you and ¹_____? Adventure camp is great. It's my third day here. I have some new friends from ²_____ and Mexico. They're really nice. I'm teaching ³_____ to my new friend, Flo. She's funny. I like her, but she's not good at learning Spanish!

Our first day was good. There was a big dinner, and then there were songs by the campfire. I don't like ⁴_____, but it was fun. Bed was late. Tonight I want to go to bed early!

Yesterday, we ⁵_____ for a walk in the forest. It's very beautiful here. There ⁶_____ any computers, and there ⁷_____ any Internet, but I ⁸_____ the camp.

Felipe

18 **Write.**

1   Who is the letter for?

_____

2   Is it Felipe's second day?

_____

3   What did Felipe do yesterday?

_____

19 Write.

20 Write. Use the words from Activity 19.

1 Bear Grylls usually lives in the United Kingdom, but sometimes he lives in the desert, the _____, or the jungle.

2 Bear Grylls likes playing the _____.

3 There are often a lot of _____ and insects in the jungle.

4 Bear Grylls sometimes sleeps up in a _____ in the jungle.

5 His favorite place is an _____ in Indonesia.

6 Bear Grylls runs a lot and does _____.

7 The _____ is a difficult place to live in.

8 Bear Grylls is a _____ and an adventurer.

21 **Match.**

1	poles		**a**	This tells you where north is.
2	tent		**b**	You do this to sleep on the floor.
3	sleeping bag		**c**	You use this to see in the dark.
4	pegs		**d**	This keeps you warm at night.
5	flashlight		**e**	You do this to start a fire.
6	set up the bed		**f**	a house you can take with you
7	cover		**g**	You can carry clothes and books in this.
8	light		**h**	You use these to stop a tent from flying away.
9	compass		**i**	You use these to support a tent.
10	backpack		**j**	put something over something

22 **Listen, circle, and number.**

Ron

Jo

Brad

Jackie

a I can pitch a tent, (but / and) I (can / can't) read a compass. ☐

b I like lighting fires, (but / and) I (like / don't like) cooking. ☐

c I love hiking with a flashlight at night, (but / and) I (love / don't love) camping under the stars. ☐

d I (like / don't like) walking in the rain, (but / and) I usually cover my head. ☐

23 **Unscramble and write. Then write *Yes* or *No* for you.**

1 mom / tennis / at / good / my / playing / is

_____ Is it true? _____

2 like swimming / I / I / don't like running / but

_____ Is it true? _____

3 loves / my / fishing / father

_____ Is it true? _____

24 **Listen and write.**

Two people I love are my mother and my brother. My ¹_____ is good

at baseball. He plays every day. My ²_____ isn't good at baseball. She

can't throw and ³_____ hit. She ⁴_____ sporty. She loves

⁵_____ romantic books and likes ⁶_____ dramas on TV. My brother

⁷_____ like romantic movies or books, ⁸_____ he loves action

movies. He isn't ⁹_____ math, and my mom can't ¹⁰_____ because

she isn't good at math, either!

25 **Write about two people.**

What are they good at? What do they like doing? What do they love doing?

What are they not good at? What don't they like doing?

Two people I love are _____ and _____.

_____

_____

_____

_____

_____

_____

_____

_____

 Are you ready for Unit 2?

2 Wildlife park

1 **Unscramble and write. Then match.**

a

b

c

d

e

f

1	trote	_____
2	takerem	_____
3	sale	_____
4	eas tutelr	_____
5	iponrosc	_____
6	hcthaee	_____
7	melur	_____
8	retpahn	_____
9	alkoa	_____
10	mue	_____
11	oinrh	_____
12	egrit	_____
13	eawlh	_____

g

h

i

j

k

l

m

2 **Write about the animals in Activity 1.**

| big | fast | heavy | scary | slow |

1 <u>Cheetahs are fast.</u>

2 _____

4 _____

3 _____

5 _____

3 **Listen and write. Then match.**

1 <u>   210   </u>

2 _____

3 _____

4 _____

5 _____

a two thousand ten

b three hundred seventy

c six hundred forty-two

d one thousand eighteen

e four thousand seventeen

4 **Listen and write.**

		How tall?	How heavy?	How long?
①		1.2 meters	___250___ kilograms	2.5 meters
②		_____ meters	60 kilograms	_____ meters
③			_____ kilograms	_____ meters
④		_____ meters	_____ kilograms	_____ meters
⑤		_____ meters	_____ kilograms	_____ meters

5 **Unscramble and write questions.**

1 hippo / is / long / how / the   _____

2 tall / how / lion / is / the   _____

3 the / heavy / snake / how / is   _____

4 long / how / is / the / elephant   _____

5 cheetah / how / tall / is / the   _____

6 **Look at Activity 4 and write answers to the questions in Activity 5.**

1   <u>The hippo is 4 meters long.</u>

2   _____

3   _____

4   _____

5   _____

7 Write.

1 big   <u>bigger</u>   <u>biggest</u>   **2** tall   _____   _____

3 heavy   _____   _____   **4** slow   _____   _____

5 short   _____   _____   **6** small   _____   _____

7 fast   _____   _____   **8** light   _____   _____

9 long   _____   _____

8 Write.

1 The lemur <u>is faster than the tiger</u> _____. (fast)

2 The panther _____. (big)

3 The whale _____. (long)

4 The whale _____. (heavy)

5 The seal _____. (small)

6 The turtle _____. (slow)

9 Write questions. Then look at Activity 8 and write the answers.

1 panther / fast / lemur

<u>Is the panther faster than the lemur?</u>   <u>No, it isn't.</u>

2 turtle / fast / otter

_____   _____

3 whale / heavy / sea turtle

_____   _____

10 Write.

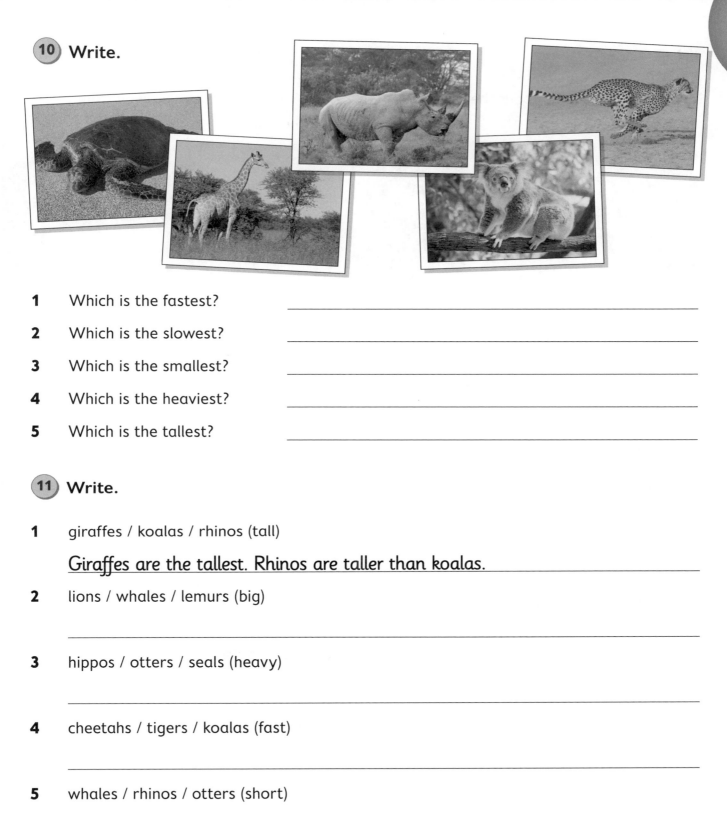

1 Which is the fastest? _____

2 Which is the slowest? _____

3 Which is the smallest? _____

4 Which is the heaviest? _____

5 Which is the tallest? _____

11 Write.

1 giraffes / koalas / rhinos (tall)

Giraffes are the tallest. Rhinos are taller than koalas. _____

2 lions / whales / lemurs (big)

_____

3 hippos / otters / seals (heavy)

_____

4 cheetahs / tigers / koalas (fast)

_____

5 whales / rhinos / otters (short)

_____

6 elephants / koalas / gorillas (light)

_____

12 Check (✓).

1 Who knows a lot about the animals they meet?

 a  b  c

2 Who helps Matt get away from the rhino?

 a  b  c

13 Correct the sentences.

1 The rhino is the fastest animal they see.

_____

2 Bella calls the cheetah "little guy."

_____

3 They talk to the mysterious couple.

_____

14 Write. Then number the story events in order.

> arrive   climb   leave   running   says   sees   ties

☐ Matt _____ a cheetah.

☐ They all _____ Africa quickly.

☐ Bella _____ "hi" to a meerkat.

☐ Matt and Bella _____ a tree.

☐ Bella _____ a knot in her rope, and they get down from the tree.

☐ Matt, Bella, and AL _____ in Africa.

☐ The mysterious couple are _____ away from a rhino.

15 Write.

	1	2	3
Situation A You're planning a birthday party for a friend. What's the easiest way to invite everyone?	Send text messages to all your friends. (You don't have all the cell phone numbers.)	Put up a notice on the school noticeboard with date, place, and time.	Send everyone a message online. Not everyone is online. You invite these people tomorrow at school.
_____ is easier than _____. _____ is the _____.			
Situation B You're near a river, and a friend falls into the water. He can't swim. You can't swim. What's the smartest thing to do?	Jump into the river.	Call for help and wait for someone to arrive.	Call for help. You find a tree branch and try to help your friend.
_____ is smarter than _____. _____ is the _____.			
Situation C An old friend is in town. You want to do something this weekend. What's the best thing to do?	Invite your friend to dinner at your home. You ask your family first.	Plan a party at your home with two other friends. You don't ask your family first.	Plan a guided tour of your city with friends. You ask your family first.
_____ is better than _____. _____ is the _____.			

16 **Write about a decision you made and how you made it.**

1 I decided to _____.

_____

2 Was it a good decision? Why?

_____

17 **Listen and circle.**

1 Mike (likes / doesn't like) the koala reserve.

2 Vernie is (7 meters / 70 centimeters) tall.

3 Vernie likes (running / sleeping).

4 Vernie is (8 / 80) kilograms.

5 Mike wants to sponsor (Jen / Vernie).

18 **Listen again and number the questions in order. Then write the answers.**

a How tall is Vernie? ☐ _____

b Can I ask you some questions? ☐ _____

c Can she run? ☐ _____

d How heavy is she? ☐ _____

e How fast is she? ☐ _____

f Do you like the koala reserve? ☐ _____

g So, why all the questions? ☐ _____

19 **Write. Then circle T = True, F = False, or S = Sometimes.**

1 Giraffes are _____taller_____ (tall) than lions. T / F / S

2 Rhinos are _____ (heavy) than cheetahs. T / F / S

3 Cheetahs are _____ (short) than elephants. T / F / S

4 Sea turtles are _____ (big) than whales. T / F / S

5 Crocodiles are _____ (long) than snakes. T / F / S

6 Elephants are _____ (slow) than cheetahs. T / F / S

7 Seals are _____ (small) than rabbits. T / F / S

8 Monkeys are _____ (light) than whales. T / F / S

9 Turtles are _____ (fast) than gorillas. T / F / S

20 **Listen and write.**

Cool camouflage in the cold!

Size They are not very heavy, and they are not very big. Their tails are usually about 30 centimeters long.

Body Arctic foxes have short legs and short ears. Their coats and tails are very thick and warm — good for living in the snow!

Color Their coats are very good camouflage. They are white when it is snowy in the winter. In the summer, their coats are darker and change to brown or gray. It is difficult to see the foxes next to the brown rocks.

Places Arctic foxes live only in the Arctic, for example, in Canada and Greenland. It is very cold there. They can live in temperatures of -50 degrees Celsius.

Food Arctic foxes eat birds, fish, and sometimes vegetables. They are good at catching birds — they are very fast! They often put food in the snow and then eat it later in the year.

1 Arctic foxes have white coats in _____.

2 Arctic foxes have brown coats in _____.

21 **Write c (chameleon) or f (fox).**

1 This animal changes color when it is nervous. ☐

2 This animal lives in very cold places. ☐

3 This animal sometimes eats fish. ☐

4 This animal has a very long tongue. ☐

22 **Think about a wild animal that uses camouflage. Write and draw.**

Animal		Size	
Body		Color	
Places		Food	

23 Match.

1	heavy	**a**	opposite of slow
2	short	**b**	an Australian animal that some people think is cute
3	tall	**c**	opposite of long
4	fast	**d**	an animal that can't walk but is good at swimming
5	camouflage	**e**	a good swimmer that lives in rivers and has a long tail
6	sea turtle	**f**	a water animal that has a hard shell
7	otter	**g**	Animals use this for safety.
8	seal	**h**	opposite of light
9	tiger	**i**	a cat with striped fur
10	koala	**j**	opposite of short

24 Circle.

1 How (heavy / heavier) is the elephant? It's 2,000 (kilograms / meters).

2 How (long / longer) is it? It's 2.5 meters (long / longer).

3 The panther is (bigger / biggest) than the koala.

4 The sea turtle is the (shorter / shortest).

5 Are giraffes (taller / tallest) than otters? (Yes, they are. / No, they aren't.)

6 Are rhinos (heavy / heavier) than lemurs? (Yes, they are. / No, they aren't.)

7 Are panthers (faster / fastest) than cheetahs? (Yes, they are. / No, they aren't.)

8 Are lemurs (small / smaller) than whales? (Yes, they are. / No, they aren't.)

25 Read and number.

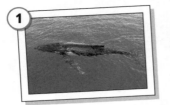   

a Which is the heaviest land animal in the world? ☐

b Which is the tallest animal in the world? ☐

c Which is the fastest land animal in the world? ☐

d Which is the longest animal in the world? ☐

26  **Listen and write.**

My favorite animal is the hippo. At the ¹_____ I can watch the hippos for

an hour! They are really ²_____ animals. When they walk, they are very

³_____. ⁴_____ heavy is a hippo? One hippo weighs between

1,500 and 3,000 ⁵_____. Hippos are the third ⁶_____ animals in

the world (elephants and rhinos are ⁷_____ than hippos). Hippos can swim.

They are ⁸_____ swimmers, and they look beautiful in the water. Hippos

enjoy water and having baths. They have small ears but very big mouths and big

⁹_____. A hippo's mouth is ¹⁰_____.

27 **Write about your favorite animal.**

_____

_____

_____

_____

_____

_____

_____

_____

_____

_____

⭐ **Are you ready for Unit 3?**

Lesson 10

3 Where we live

1 Write the places. Then find.

1

_____

2

_____

3

_____

4

_____

5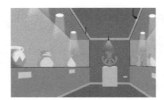

_____

6

_____

s	h	o	p	p	i	n	g	m	a	l	l	k	n	l
r	e	s	r	m	f	a	q	s	t	p	j	c	p	f
l	t	d	c	r	q	l	a	g	y	u	d	b	a	e
i	w	m	o	v	i	e	t	h	e	a	t	e	r	m
b	u	v	s	x	w	i	o	h	z	h	i	c	k	d
r	v	n	i	q	b	y	p	g	k	z	v	a	n	o
a	s	c	r	m	u	s	e	u	m	o	p	l	e	y
r	a	j	t	i	x	k	h	l	m	g	b	w	x	f
y	p	u	s	u	p	e	r	m	a	r	k	e	t	o

2 Write. Use the words from Activity 1.

1 I can buy juice in a _____.

2 I can find interesting books in a _____.

3 I can have a picnic in a _____.

4 I can see old things in a _____.

5 I can watch a movie in a _____.

6 I can buy some clothes in a _____.

3 🎧 **Listen and write.**

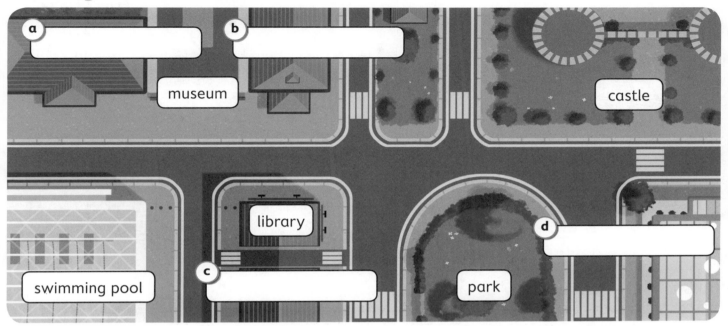

- **a** [_____]
- **b** [_____]
- museum
- castle
- library
- swimming pool
- **c** [_____]
- **d** [_____]
- park

4 **Look at the map in Activity 3 and write.**

1 museum / school   The museum is next to the school. _____

2 bank / library   _____

3 museum / supermarket / school   _____

4 shopping mall / castle   _____

5 supermarket / museum / swimming pool   _____

5 **Write directions from the nearest bus stop to your home.**

Get off the bus and _____

_____

6 Write.

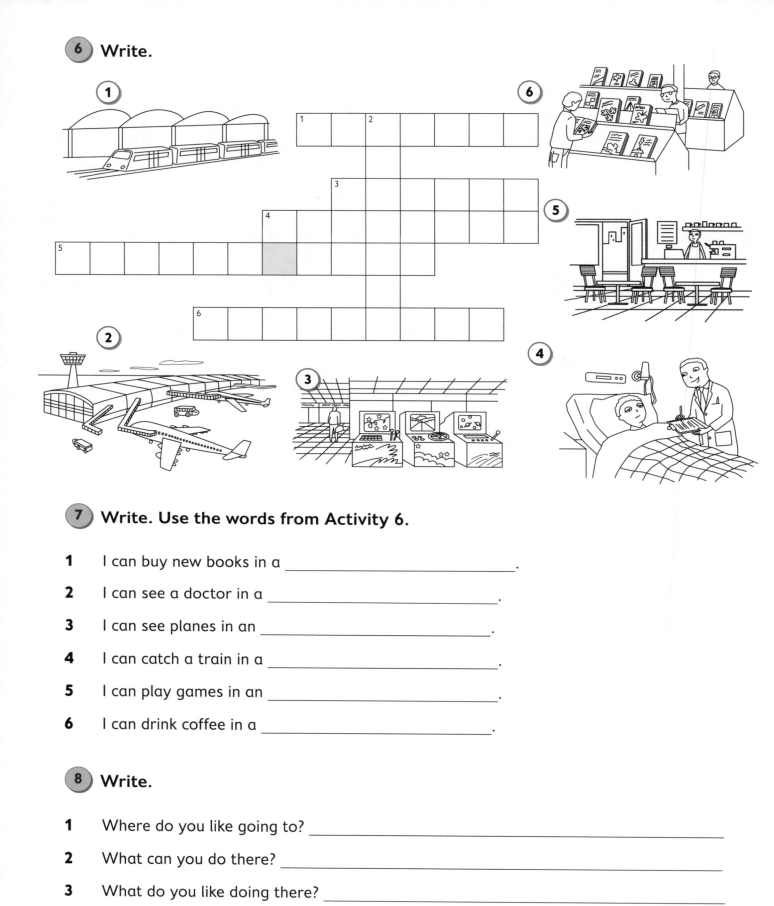

7 Write. Use the words from Activity 6.

1 I can buy new books in a _____.

2 I can see a doctor in a _____.

3 I can see planes in an _____.

4 I can catch a train in a _____.

5 I can play games in an _____.

6 I can drink coffee in a _____.

8 Write.

1 Where do you like going to? _____

2 What can you do there? _____

3 What do you like doing there? _____

9 **Write.**

1 Tom / go / park / ✗

<u>Tom doesn't want to go to the park.</u>

2 Flo / meet / in town for lunch / Sunday / ✓

_____

3 Felipe / see / a movie / Saturday / ✗

_____

4 Maria / play basketball / this afternoon / ✓

_____

10 **Look at Activity 9 and write the questions. Then listen and write the answers.**

1 Hi, Tom. <u>Do you want to go to</u> <u>the park?</u>
_____

No, sorry. <u>I have to go</u> <u>shopping to buy a new</u> <u>computer.</u>

2 Hi, Flo. _____
_____
_____

Yes, _____ .
_____
_____

3 Hi, Felipe. _____
_____
_____

No, sorry. I have _____
_____ .
_____

4 Hi, Maria. _____
_____
_____

No, sorry. _____
_____
_____

11 Check (✓).

1 Who wants to go to the control center?

2 Who sees that someone is coming?

12 Circle.

1 AL (knows / doesn't know) what Dot and Zeb Martin are looking for.

2 Dot and Zeb Martin are trying to (buy / take) a space-time chip.

3 Matt wants to (eat something / find something).

13 Complete the summary.

> Atlantis   chip   control center   hungry   security guard   time-travel

Zeb and Dot Martin go to ^{1}_____. Matt, Bella, and AL follow them. They see a video of the Martins in the ^{2}_____. AL says the Martins are looking for a space-time ^{3}_____. The chip is important for a ^{4}_____ machine. A ^{5}_____ comes, and they hide. Matt is ^{6}_____, and he thinks the Martins are, too.

14 **Find and write.**

VALUES

Learn to be flexible. It can be frustrating when you have to do things you don't want to do. Learn to stay calm and just do it!

I want to... **but I have to...**

1 I want to ___meet my friends___, but I have to go to ___the supermarket___ with my dad.

2 I want to go to the _____, but _____ take my little brother to _____.

3 _____ play _____ go to _____.

4 _____ go to _____.

5 _____ study for _____.

15 🎧 **Listen and number the sentences in order.**

a Do you want to come to Seoul in the summer? ☐

b I don't like quiet places! ☐

c I live near a big park with a lot of trees and flowers. ☐

d I want to be good at everything! ☐

e Thanks for your email. It was really interesting! ☐

Alex

Sun-kwan

16 🎧 **Circle. Then listen again and check your answers.**

1 Alex (wants / doesn't want) to know more about Seoul.

2 Sun-kwan (likes / doesn't like) quiet places.

3 There's a river (opposite / behind) Sun-kwan's house.

4 Sun-kwan (wants / doesn't want) to go to Sark one day.

17 **Write and, but, or because.**

1 I don't like the city _____ it's too noisy.

2 She wants to go to bed _____ she's tired.

3 He likes going to the library, _____ he doesn't like going to the castle.

4 My town is clean, _____ it isn't beautiful.

5 I like surfing _____ snorkeling.

18 **Write about where you live.**

I like my city because _____.

In _____ there are _____ and _____.

There are _____, but there aren't any _____.

19 Write.

bridge   chimney   hill   river   roof

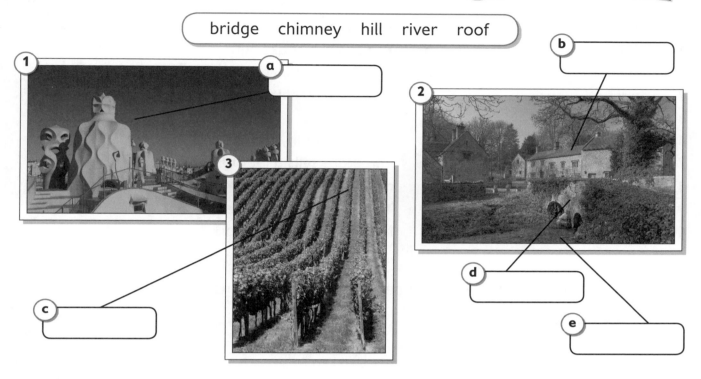

20 Look at Activity 19. Number. Then write.

Australia   because   bridge   houses
near   next   park   summer   village

☐ **a** Upper Swell is a pretty ¹_____ in the United Kingdom. It has a lot of old

²_____. There is also a river in the village with a ³_____.

You can sit and watch the water. It is very quiet, but a lot of people visit it in the

⁴_____.

☐ **b** The Adelaide Hills are in ⁵_____. It is very beautiful there. You can see

a lot of animals and birds in the wildlife ⁶_____. The hills are

⁷_____ the city of Adelaide.

☐ **c** Barcelona is a big city in Spain, ⁸_____ to the water. It has a lot

of interesting buildings. Tourists ⁹_____ to go there ¹⁰_____

there is always a lot to do and see. This building is by Gaudi. Do you like it?

21 **Match.**

1	library		**a**	You can fly from here.
2	behind		**b**	You can get books here.
3	supermarket		**c**	You can play video games here.
4	park		**d**	You can play catch here.
5	hospital		**e**	not far away
6	airport		**f**	There are many trains here.
7	arcade		**g**	This store sells a lot of food.
8	station		**h**	opposite of "in front of"
9	bank		**i**	You can get money here.
10	near		**j**	Nurses and doctors work here.

22 🎧 **Listen and write the places. Then write the answers.**
24

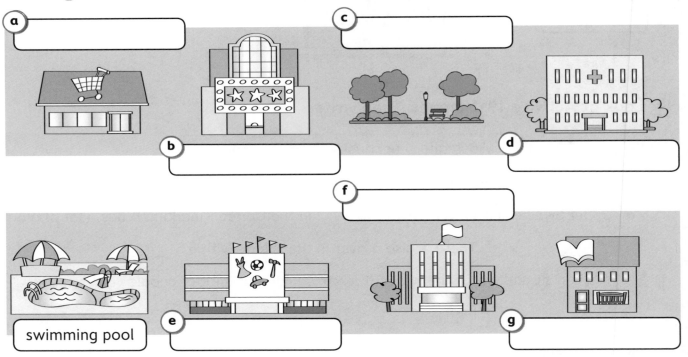

a _____

b _____

c _____

d _____

e _____

f _____

g _____

swimming pool

Where does she have to go?

1 She has to _____.

2 _____

Where does she want to go?

3 _____

4 _____

23 **Listen and write.**

I live in a small town, but I like it. There aren't any shopping malls or movie theaters,

but there ¹_____ some restaurants and a lot of ²_____ stores.

One good Chinese ³_____ is ⁴_____ my house. There is a

supermarket, too. It is ⁵_____ the swimming pool. I ⁶_____ to

go to the swimming pool tomorrow with my friends. There is a ⁷_____,

too. Sometimes I go there to get books. The library is near my school – go

straight from my house and ⁸_____ left. There is a small food store

⁹_____ my house, too. It is open late, so I can ¹⁰_____ get things

when I want them.

24 **Write about where you live.**

_____

_____

_____

_____

_____

_____

_____

_____

_____

 Are you ready for Unit 4?

Good days, bad days

1 Write. What is Flo's favorite food?

My favorite food is _____ .

2 Complete the quiz. Use the words from Activity 1.

Quiz

1 <u>Spaghetti</u>_____ is Italian.   Do you eat it?   Yes / No

2 _____ is Spanish.   Do you eat it?   Yes / No

3 _____ is Indian.   Do you eat it?   Yes / No

4 _____ is British.   Do you eat it?   Yes / No

5 _____ is Japanese.   Do you eat it?   Yes / No

6 _____ are Chinese.   Do you eat them?   Yes / No

3 **Write.**

1 climb <u> climbed </u>   **2** cook _____   **3** drop _____

4 want _____   **5** paddle _____   **6** fall _____

7 sail _____   **8** eat _____

4 **Write. Use words from Activity 3.**

1    **2**    **3**

I _____ Mount Everest last year.

We _____ paella yesterday. It was difficult!

He _____ the plate on his foot. Ouch!

5 **Write. Then circle.**

ate   loved   omelets   paddled   wanted   was   went

Yesterday was a good day! A lot of people ¹_____ to the lake to do

sports, and I went with them. There was swimming, snorkeling, and kayaking.

I ²_____ scared at first, but I ³_____ kayaking. It was exciting!

I ⁴_____ to do it all day. I was with Tom, and we ⁵_____ very

quickly around the lake. There was a race with Flo and Maria, and Tom was the

winner.

After our day at the lake, we had ⁶_____ and salad for dinner.

I ⁷_____ my dinner very quickly because I was really hungry!

Who is the writer?   Tom / Flo / Felipe

6 **Circle. Then match.**

1 miss (the bus / the bag)

2 eat (my juice / my lunch)

3 drop (the ball / the bus)

4 pass (a test / a curry)

5 pack (my test / my bag)

6 bring (my juice / my home)

7 **Circle.**

1 They were very hungry this morning, so they (ate / didn't eat) some sandwiches.

2 Flo (missed / didn't miss) the bus yesterday. She was early.

3 Tom (dropped / didn't drop) the ball. He caught it.

4 Felipe (brought / didn't bring) his lunch. He had to buy lunch.

5 Last night, I (packed / didn't pack) my bag. I always pack it early.

6 I (passed / didn't pass) my science test last week. I'm good at science.

8 **Write.**

1 The woman _____ (not like) the movie, but the boys _____ (love) it.

2 He _____ (not play) soccer last week. He was sad because he really _____ (want) to play.

3 She _____ (put) a lot of food on her tray, but she _____ (not drop) her lunch.

9   **Listen and number.**

a

b

c

d

10 **Look at the pictures in Activity 9. Write the answers.**

a What happened? _____

b What happened? _____

c What happened? _____

d What happened? _____

11 **Write about yourself.**

> brought/didn't bring   passed/didn't pass   missed/didn't miss   dropped/caught

1 _____

2 _____

3 _____

4 _____

12 Check (✓).

1 Who didn't eat any food?

2 Who didn't like the meerkat?

13 Correct the sentences.

1 Zeb didn't like the dumplings.

_____

2 Dot knew what the meerkat was.

_____

3 Dot and Zeb didn't take the trash can of old food.

_____

14 Write. Then number the story events in order.

asked   ate   left   looked   made   thought

☐ Dot _____ in a trash can.

☐ Dot _____ the meerkat was a rat.

☐ Matt, Bella, and the meerkat _____ some food.

☐ Dot and Zeb _____ the restaurant with the trash can.

☐ Dee _____ dumplings for Zeb.

☐ Zeb _____ Dot what happened.

15 Write. What should they do?

VALUES

Be positive about your day.
Don't worry. Be happy.

call a friend   do some exercise
eat something you like   go swimming
go to the movies   meet some friends   play some games   relax
rest   stay home   take a shower   talk to someone   watch TV

1

I took a test today. I have a bad headache.

You should take a shower and rest.

_____

2

I studied math all day. I hate math!

_____

_____

3

I worked all day. My neck and shoulders hurt.

_____

_____

4

I worked all day. I need a break.

_____

_____

5

I got excellent grades today. I want to celebrate.

_____

_____

16 **Listen and match.**

1 Amy

2 Mark

3 David

a   I went on vacation with my family.

b   My family planned a party for me.

c   I passed the test.

17 **Listen again and circle.**

1   Amy didn't want...

    a a party.   **b** a big party.   **c** a surprise party.

2   Amy's mom cooked...

    a omelets.   **b** curry.   **c** spaghetti.

3   Mark's test was...

    a geography.   **b** Spanish.   **c** math.

4   Mark's friends...

    a passed the test.   **b** didn't pass the test.   **c** missed the test.

5   David went...

    a swimming and sailing.   **b** swimming and surfing.   **c** swimming and kayaking.

18 **Write.**

1   He _____ to go to the park yesterday. He stayed home. (not want)

2   They always _____ dinner at six o'clock. (cook)

3   I _____ the movie, but it was too long. (enjoy)

4   We always _____ our tests because we always do our homework. (pass)

5   She _____ the bus because she was late. (miss)

19 Write.

> dangerous   filmed   funny   laughed   presents   storms

1   sailed, started, finished, called, enjoyed, _____, _____

2   scary, brave, boring, tired, sad, _____, _____

3   sailor, world, journey, waves, family, _____, _____

20 Write.

Yesterday was a really good day. There were no  ¹ _____,

and the weather was good. I was  ² _____ because

I  ³ _____ my family and friends. I ⁴ _____

my Christmas presents, too. I ⁵ _____ the funny presents and

the ⁶ _____ .

21 Imagine you're a sailor or explorer. Circle. Then write about a good day or a bad day.

> exciting   happy   jungle   mountains   ocean   sad   scary   storm

Yesterday was a (good / bad) day. _____

_____

_____

22 Match.

1	curry	**a**	You use eggs to make this.
2	dumplings	**b**	a hot and spicy food that is from India
3	stew	**c**	opposite of catch
4	pack	**d**	fish and rice – popular in Japan
5	spaghetti	**e**	rice and seafood – popular in Spain
6	drop	**f**	a Chinese food
7	fish and chips	**g**	a dish of meat and vegetables cooked slowly
8	sushi	**h**	a type of pasta
9	paella	**i**	put things in a bag
10	omelet	**j**	a popular food in the United Kingdom

23 Listen and number. Then write.

a She _____ yesterday.

b They _____ a big _____ last year.

c We _____ stew for _____ today.

24 Unscramble and write. Then match.

1 didn't / he / the / bus / miss

_____

a because it wasn't sunny.

2 didn't / sunglasses / bring / my / I

_____

b because he got up early.

3 catch / she / the / baseball / didn't

_____

c because it was very fast.

46 Lesson 9

25   **Listen and write.**

Last weekend was sunny. We ¹_____ soccer. We didn't win because our

goalkeeper ²_____ the ball many times, and we ³_____ many

chances to score. After the game, I ⁴_____ home with my friends to have

dinner. My mom ⁵_____ stew and spaghetti. We ⁶_____ a lot of

food. We ⁷_____ about the game and ⁸_____ our plan for the

next game.

26 **Write about what happened to you last weekend or last night.**

    Are you ready for Unit 5?

5 Trips

1 Write.

_____

_____

_____

_____

_____

_____

_____

_____

2 Write. Use words from Activity 1.

1   We went to the _____. There were a lot of fish there.

2   The _____ was great. We camped on Friday and Saturday night.

3   We loved the _____ because we love swimming.

4   I liked the _____. It was inside a big tent, and there were funny people.

5   The _____ was great. I really liked the actors.

6   The _____ was fun. I was sometimes scared, but it was exciting!

7   The _____ was fun, but the queen wasn't there.

8   There were a lot of amazing trees and flowers at the _____.

3 Write about yourself. Use words from Activity 1.

I love going to the _____ and _____.

I like _____,

but I don't _____.

4 Write.

1 I _____ Ping-Pong last Wednesday.

2 They _____ to the amusement park on Saturday.

3 No, she _____.

4 He didn't _____ to the park yesterday.

> didn't
> go
> played
> went

5 Look at Activity 4 and write the questions.

1 _____ you do last week?

2 What did they _____?

3 _____ to the swimming pool?

4 _____ to the _____?

6 Unscramble and write.

1 the / yesterday / did / go / you / to / supermarket

_____

2 went / ago / she / sports stadium / the / to / days / two

_____

3 on / the / didn't / bookstore / we / go / to / Saturday

_____

7 🎧 Listen and ✓ or ✗. Then write questions and answers.

| 1 | 2 | 3 | 4 |

1 <u>Did Maria go to the palace?</u>   <u>Yes, she did.</u>

2 _____   _____

3 _____   _____

4 _____   _____

8 Write. Then find.

1 _____

2 _____

a	r	o	l	l	e	r	c	o	a	s	t	e	r
p	m	i	n	i	a	t	u	r	e	g	o	l	f
i	z	b	s	e	r	c	f	p	q	j	d	i	g
r	b	f	e	r	r	i	s	w	h	e	e	l	k
a	u	s	a	r	e	m	v	a	w	y	z	t	k
t	m	n	y	g	o	s	d	t	c	l	u	s	c
e	p	k	a	q	a	h	i	e	e	d	h	n	l
s	e	i	h	g	b	c	p	r	o	u	s	e	n
h	r	l	p	f	n	x	d	s	o	b	e	v	t
i	c	m	z	n	f	w	m	l	f	b	n	k	j
p	a	w	q	t	b	k	u	i	r	g	u	p	x
x	r	o	v	y	j	c	u	d	l	v	m	w	t
p	s	z	p	a	d	d	l	e	b	o	a	t	s

3 _____

4 _____

5 _____

9 There are two more places in Activity 8.
Find them and write.

> My favorite ride is the _____.
> I also like playing _____ with my friends.

10 Write. Then match.

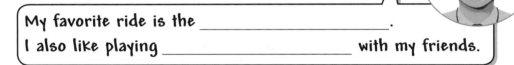

go   like   play   watch

1 Did they _____ the chocolate cake?

a No, they didn't. They saw a scary one.

2 Did they _____ soccer yesterday?

b Yes, they did. They loved the fish.

3 Did they _____ to the aquarium?

c No, they didn't. It was too rainy.

4 Did they _____ a funny movie?

d Yes, they did. They loved it!

11 **Match.**

1   What will you do at the library?

2   What will you do at the bank?

3   What will you do at the sports stadium?

4   What will you do at the museum?

5   What will you do at the aquarium?

6   What will you do at the national park?

a   I'll get some money.

b   First, I'll get some books for school. Then I'll check the Internet.

c   First, I'll go to the dinosaur room. Then I'll go to the insect room.

d   I'll see a lot of beautiful fish.

e   First, I'll pitch the tent. Then I'll go kayaking.

f   I'll watch a soccer game.

12 **Write.**

horseback riding   in-line skating   rock climbing
skateboarding   ~~snorkeling~~   surfing

1

First, I'll go **snorkeling** _____

_____ .

Then I'll go _____

_____ .

2

First, _____

_____ .

Then _____

_____ .

3

_____

_____

_____

_____

13 Check (✓).

1   Who was not happy at the beginning of the story?

2   Who said that Dot and Zeb used the THD for power?

14 Answer the questions.

1   Did Matt and AL fly in the space pod?

_____

2   Did Carol see a flash and hear a bang?

_____

3   Did Bella find the pod?

_____

15 Listen and number.

a   water park ☐   **b**   palace ☐

c   aquarium ☐   **d**   amusement park ☐

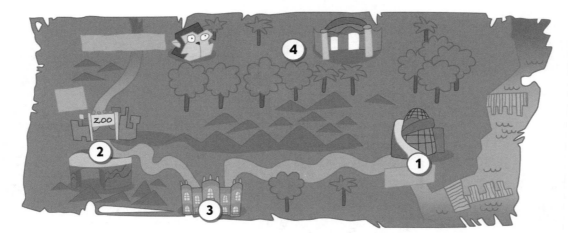

16 **Read Felipe's schedule. Then write.**

Time	To do:
7:30	get up, shower, and have breakfast
8:30	meet friends in front of the camp
8:45	take a bus to the water park - go swimming - go on the water slide
12:00	have lunch
2:00	go to amusement park - ride the roller coaster - play miniature golf
5:00	take bus back to camp

Tomorrow is the big day! We'll go to the water park and amusement park!

At 7:30, I'll get up, shower, and have breakfast.

At 8:30, [1]_____

friends [2]_____ the camp.

Then, at 8:45, [3]_____ take

a bus to the [4]_____.

First, we'll [5]_____.

Then we'll [6]_____. At 12:00, we'll [7]_____.

At 2:00, we'll [8]_____. [9]_____,

we'll [10]_____. [11]_____

we'll [12]_____. At 5:00, we'll take the bus back to the camp.

17 **Plan how to review for an English test. Number in the best order.**

a   Ask a friend to review.   ☐

b   Plan the work, and when and where to meet.   ☐

c   Read the "Look" boxes and check we understand them.   ☐

d   Find examples of the grammar in each unit.   ☐

e   Meet at the school library.   ☐

18 **Write.**

amusement park   go   have to   jump on the trampoline   will

Come to Adventure World!

You ¹_____ love Adventure

World! You will like our long, sandy beaches!

You ²_____ visit the famous

³_____! In the evening,

go in-line skating or ⁴_____!

You will never want to ⁵_____ home!

19  **Listen and circle.**

1   Oliver went to the (water park / amusement park).

2   The rides were (boring / exciting).

3   The weather was (rainy / sunny).

4   Oliver went (on the trampoline / in-line skating).

20 **Write about your plan for your next vacation.**

On my next vacation with my family, we'll _____.

First, we'll _____.

Then _____.

After that, _____.

I'll be sure to have a great time.

21 Circle and write your scores.

How beach-safe are you?

1 When it is sunny on the beach, you always wear a...
   a bracelet.
   b watch.
   c hat. ☐

2 When you go to the beach, you always...
   a bring sunblock.
   b eat ice cream.
   c wear your favorite jeans. ☐

3 When swimming in the sea, you...
   a always swim near the beach.
   b always swim far from the beach.
   c never swim near the beach. ☐

4 Before swimming in the sea, you...
   a always find the safe flags.
   b wash your face.
   c sometimes find the safe flags. ☐

5 When surfing in the sea, your surfboard is always...
   a on the beach.
   b next to you.
   c far from you. ☐

1 a 0 points   b 0 points   c 5 points
2 a 5 points   b 0 points   c 0 points
3 a 5 points   b 0 points   c 0 points
4 a 5 points   b 0 points   c 0 points
5 a 0 points   b 5 points   c 0 points
20–25 points: You are very safe on the beach!
10–20 points: You are quite safe, but read the rules again!
0–10 points: Oh, no! Don't go to the beach!

22 Write safety rules for the beach.

1 You should _____.

2 _____

3 _____

4 _____

23 **Match.**

1	bumper cars	**a**	You can ride these on a lake.
2	aquarium	**b**	You can sail in this but not on the ocean.
3	paddle boats	**c**	This is a big natural area in the mountains or forest.
4	amusement park	**d**	Children can drive these.
5	roller coaster	**e**	A king or queen lives here.
6	circus	**f**	This is fast and wet!
7	pirate ship	**g**	You can see many types of fish here.
8	national park	**h**	This is a fast and exciting ride but not wet.
9	water slide	**i**	This is usually in a big tent.
10	palace	**j**	This is a fun place. There are many rides here.

24 **Write.**

1 What did you do yesterday?

_____

2 What will you do tomorrow?

First, _____ .

Then _____ .

25 **Unscramble and write questions. Then write the answers.**

1 supermarket / did / go / to / a / you / yesterday

_____

_____

2 mom / week / did / go / to / last / theater / your / a

_____

_____

3 did / a / circus / year / go / to / last / your / friend

_____

_____

26 **Listen and write.**

Next week is our school trip. We ¹_____ on the bus at 7:30 a.m.

The bus trip ²_____ about two hours. First, we will go to a

³_____. In the museum we will study ⁴_____.

It will be interesting, I think. Then we ⁵_____ lunch in the

⁶_____ that is next to the museum. In the afternoon, we will go

to an ⁷_____. It will be a lot of fun. First, I ⁸_____ on

the ⁹_____. Then I'll go on the bumper ¹⁰_____ and

pirate ¹¹_____ with my friends. We will get home at about 8:00 p.m.

My mom is coming to school to ¹²_____ the bus.

27 **Write about somewhere you will go this year. What will you do?**

_____

_____

_____

_____

_____

_____

_____

_____

 Are you ready for Unit 6?

6 Arts

1 Write.

1

2

3

4

_____

5

6

7

8

_____

2 **Listen and circle.**

1 Maria likes (romances / thrillers) because they are exciting.

2 She thinks she's too old for (cartoons / musicals) now.

3 Felipe loves (comedies / cartoons).

4 Maria loves (musicals / comedies).

3 **Write about which types of movies you like/don't like.**

I like _____ and _____, but I don't like _____.

I love _____ because _____.

4 Write.

Last week...

1 Tom ✗ make

_____
_____

2 Maria ✓ see

_____
_____

3 Felipe ✗ have

_____
_____

4 Flo ✓ write in

_____
_____

5 Write.

| did | didn't | had | jumped | saw | was | went |

Yesterday was fun. I ¹_____ to the movie theater by myself.

I ²_____ a comedy. It was about a funny man, George.

He ³_____ many things with his dog. George always made

mistakes, but the dog corrected them. It ⁴_____ really funny.

I ⁵_____ a good time. After the movie, I saw Maria. I ⁶_____

up and down, but she ⁷_____ see me!

6 Write.

1 She went hiking by <u>herself</u>.

2 They went to school by _____.

3 You made breakfast for all the family by _____.

4 We wrote the song by _____.

5 He watched the movie by _____.

6 I played video games by _____.

7 Find and write 13 music words.

q	z	c	o	u	n	t	r	y	c	o	b
c	e	a	p	b	r	l	u	f	v	g	h
l	t	a	m	b	o	u	r	i	n	e	a
a	y	a	d	c	c	e	l	l	o	c	r
r	f	o	z	e	k	n	t	j	d	k	m
i	t	r	i	a	n	g	l	e	t	h	o
n	p	o	p	n	o	k	a	j	f	b	n
e	d	c	d	t	p	i	h	i	v	b	i
t	r	r	l	h	a	r	p	i	g	l	c
b	u	m	l	m	a	w	q	l	u	u	a
s	m	s	a	x	o	p	h	o	n	e	n
x	s	r	j	a	z	z	w	j	e	s	k

1 _____
2 _____
3 _____
4 _____
5 _____
6 _____
7 _____
8 _____
9 _____
10 _____
11 _____
12 _____
13 _____

8 Write.

> band   did   jazz   tambourine
> sang   saxophone   sing

Bryn: Did you play the clarinet at the school music festival?

Michelle: Yes, I ¹_____.

Bryn: Did Jack and John play with you in the ²_____?

Michelle: Yes, they did. Jack played the ³_____, and John played the harmonica.

We played ⁴_____ music.

Bryn: Did Alice ⁵_____? She's your singer, right?

Michelle: Yes, that's right. She ⁶_____ and hit a ⁷_____, too.

9 Look at Activity 8 and write the answers.

1   Did Michelle play at the music festival?   _____

2   What did she play?   _____

3   Did Alice play the saxophone?   _____

10   **Listen and check (✓). Then complete Flo's diary.**

	make a cake	write a birthday card	say "Happy Birthday!"	go to the theater	see dancers
Flo					
Tom					
Mom					

My birthday last year was great. My mom ¹_____ a cake for me.

Tom ²_____ a nice birthday card, and everyone ³_____

"Happy Birthday!" I was very happy. Mom ⁴_____ tickets for the

theater, and we all ⁵_____ the next day. We ⁶_____ dancers

and ⁷_____ some great music. I loved it!

11 **Write. Then listen and complete for Cho.**

		Your answer	Cho
1	Have you ever written a letter in English?		Yes, she has.
2	Have you ever bought a foreign band's CD?		
3	Have you ever made dinner for your family?		
4	Have you ever been late for school?		
5	Have you ever lost your keys?		
6	Have you ever missed a train or bus?		

12 Check (✓).

1 Who works in the recording studio?

2 Who made some music?

13 Write. Then number the story events in order.

closet   "help"   music   saxophone   studio   trace

☐ AL found a _____ and AL, Matt, and Bella left the studio.

☐ Bella, Matt, and AL arrived at the _____, but the Martins weren't there.

☐ Peter listened to the _____ that the Martins recorded.

☐ Peter told Matt that the Martins took a _____.

☐ They found Peter in a _____.

☐ They heard Peter call _____.

14 What happened in the story so far? Circle T = True or F = False.

1 Matt and AL met Bella at an adventure camp.   T / F

2 Matt and Bella talked to the Martins in Africa.   T / F

3 Dot and Zeb went to Atlantis to find a space-time chip.   T / F

4 Dot and Zeb took two food bins from the restaurant.   T / F

5 The Martins went on a ride at the amusement park.   T / F

6 Peter gave the Martins a saxophone.   T / F

15 Check *by yourself* (✓) and *as a team* (✓✓✓). Then write.

6

1

[ ] They _____

_____ as a team.

2

[ ] He _____

_____ by himself.

3

[ ] She _____

_____ .

4

[ ] He _____

_____ .

5

[ ] They _____

_____ .

6

[ ] She _____

_____ .

16 Write.

Things I like to do by myself	Things I like to do in a group
_____	_____
_____	_____
_____	_____
_____	_____
_____	_____

17 Listen and circle.

1   Alicia is talking about...

   a a song.   **b** a book.

2   The name of the book is...

   a *Inkheart.*   **b** *Inkeyes.*

3   The writer of the book is...

   a Fornelia Hunke.   **b** Cornelia Funke.

4   The name of the girl in the story is...

   a Alicia.   **b** Meggie.

 18 Listen again and check (✓).

		True	False	Don't know
1	It's about a girl, Meggie.			
2	Meggie and her dad love books.			
3	The monsters are scary.			
4	Meggie and Alicia are both 12.			
5	The book is short.			
6	Alicia didn't like the movie.			

19 Write.

> go   like   long   loved   monsters   saw   seen

1   I usually _____ to the movie theater on weekends.

2   Yesterday, I _____ the movie *Inkheart*.

3   The movie is _____, but the story is really good.

4   I _____ most of the actors in the movie.

5   I didn't _____ the actress playing Meggie.

6   I have _____ that movie.

7   The _____ in the movie are interesting.

20 Find and circle 10 words.

bedshuwfeetcbtyhereauyjdarkbneatvnjredvfysadxserkearxnhhbadmlzxtpark

21 Put the words from Activity 20 that sound the same together.

1   _____bed_____   _____red_____

2   _____   _____

3   _____   _____

4   _____   _____

5   _____   _____

22 Use the words from Activity 21. Write two-line poems.

1   I was flying over the ocean on my bed. But the ocean wasn't blue
    – it was red!

2   _____

    _____

3   _____

    _____

4   _____

    _____

5   _____

    _____

23 Match.

1	cello	**a**	You blow this instrument, and it is very small.
2	harmonica	**b**	This is a type of music that sounds like a color.
3	saxophone	**c**	A band usually has some of these. You have to hit them!
4	triangle	**d**	You can shake this or hit it.
5	blues	**e**	This is a metal instrument that you blow.
6	clarinet	**f**	This music's name sounds like a place.
7	drums	**g**	This is a large string instrument.
8	tambourine	**h**	This is a metal instrument that has three sides.
9	country	**i**	This music is popular!
10	pop	**j**	You blow into this wood instrument.

24 Number the conversation in order.

a Yes, I did.

b It was OK, but not great.

c Did you go, Mike?

d Did you two go to the GG99 concert last Saturday?

e I wanted to go, but there were no tickets.

f How was it?

25 Unscramble and write questions. Then write your answers.

1 concert / ever / played / you / a / in / music / have

_____

2 to / did / your / school / you / lunch / today / bring

_____

3 ever / concert / you / a / been / pop / have / to

_____

4 someone / you / ever / famous / met / have

_____

5 swim / ocean / summer / the / did / last / in / you

_____

26  **Listen and write.**

My ¹_____ book is *The Goblet of Fire*. This is the ²_____ book in

the Harry Potter series. I ³_____ this book a few years ⁴_____,

but I still like it. I like this book the best ⁵_____ there is a lot of action in

it, and there are a lot of battles. In this book, Harry fights a dragon by

⁶_____ – this part is really good. I ⁷_____ Harry Potter,

⁸_____ I like the character Cedric Diggory, too. Cedric Diggory was

handsome and hard-working. He was a ⁹_____ character, but he

¹⁰_____ in this book because Lord Voldemort kills him.

27 **Write a review of your favorite movie.**

_____

_____

_____

_____

_____

_____

_____

_____

_____

⭐ **Are you ready for Unit 7?**

7 Space

1 Match. Then write.

1	tele	net	**1**	_____
2	astro	ar	**2**	_____
3	space	on	**3**	_____
4	Mo	un	**4**	_____
5	pla	llite	**5**	_____
6	st	scope	**6**	_____
7	ali	naut	**7**	_____
8	co	ship	**8**	_____
9	sate	met	**9**	_____
10	S	en	**10**	_____

2 Match.

1 What is the third planet from the Sun?   **a** Mars

2 What is the second planet from the Sun?   **b** Earth

3 What is the eighth planet from the Sun?   **c** Jupiter

4 What is the fifth planet from the Sun?   **d** Neptune

5 What is the fourth planet from the Sun?   **e** Venus

3 Write.

1 The astronaut is in the _____.

2 The astronaut is angry because there are _____ in the spaceship.

3 He doesn't know _____ they got in the spaceship.

4 Alien A has a _____.

5 Alien B is _____ on the astronaut's spacesuit!

4 Unscramble and write questions. Then match to the sentences in Activity 3.

1 a / telescope / who / has

Who has a telescope? _____ ☐

2 the / is / astronaut / where

_____ ☐

3 why / astronaut / the / is / angry

_____ ☐

4 doing / Alien B / what / is

_____ ☐

5 in / how / the / get / did / aliens

_____ ☐

5 Write five questions.

1 What's the name of the biggest planet _____?

2 Where _____?

3 How _____?

4 When _____?

5 Why _____?

6 Look at the chart. Where do these words go? Write.

> complicated   difficult   exciting   frightening   important
> intelligent   kind   pretty   scary   small   smart   tall

One or two syllables [big / ea-sy]	Three syllables or more [a-ma-zing]

7 Read and ✓ or ✗ for yourself.

1 Sci-fi movies are more exciting than cartoons.

2 Soccer is more complicated than basketball.

3 Amusement parks are more amazing than national parks.

4 Elephants are more frightening than tigers.

5 Math is more important than English.

8 Unscramble and write. Then circle Yes or No.

1 more / gorgeous / than / are / movie stars

_____ singers.   Yes / No

2 Earth / fascinating / the / more / than / is

_____ other planets.   Yes / No

3 more / snakes / frightening / than / are

_____ spiders.   Yes / No

9 **Write.**

1 Who is more intelligent, astronauts or doctors?

_____

2 Which is the most important, studying, sleeping, or exercise?

_____

3 Which are less exciting, amusement parks or video games?

_____

4 Which is the least complicated, science, geography, or math?

_____

10 **Listen and write the price and weight. Then answer.**

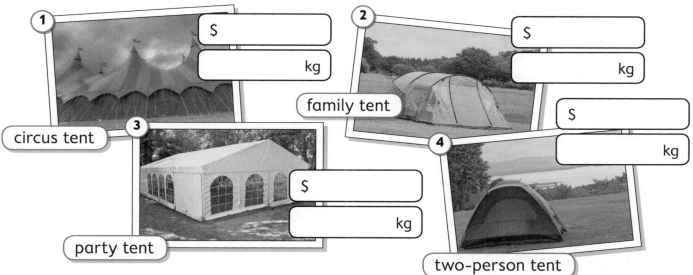

1 Which tent is the least expensive?

_____

2 Which tent is more expensive than the party tent?

_____

3 Which tent is the heaviest?

_____

4 Which tent is the lightest?

_____

11 Check (✓).

1   Who thinks they see a comet?

2   Who can't wait to go home?

12 Circle.

1   What are Zeb and Dot?

   a animals   **b** aliens   **c** astronauts

2   Dot and Zeb are happy because they found their...

   a planet.   **b** spaceship.   **c** machine.

3   What does Zeb use to start the machine?

   a his phone   **b** a computer   **c** the chip

4   What time of the day was it?

   a evening   **b** morning   **c** night

13 Unscramble and write.

> dcixeet   inzagma   eplcaticdom   ilritblan

It's _____.

She's _____.

He's _____.

She says "_____."

14 **Match and write. What materials can you use to make each model?**

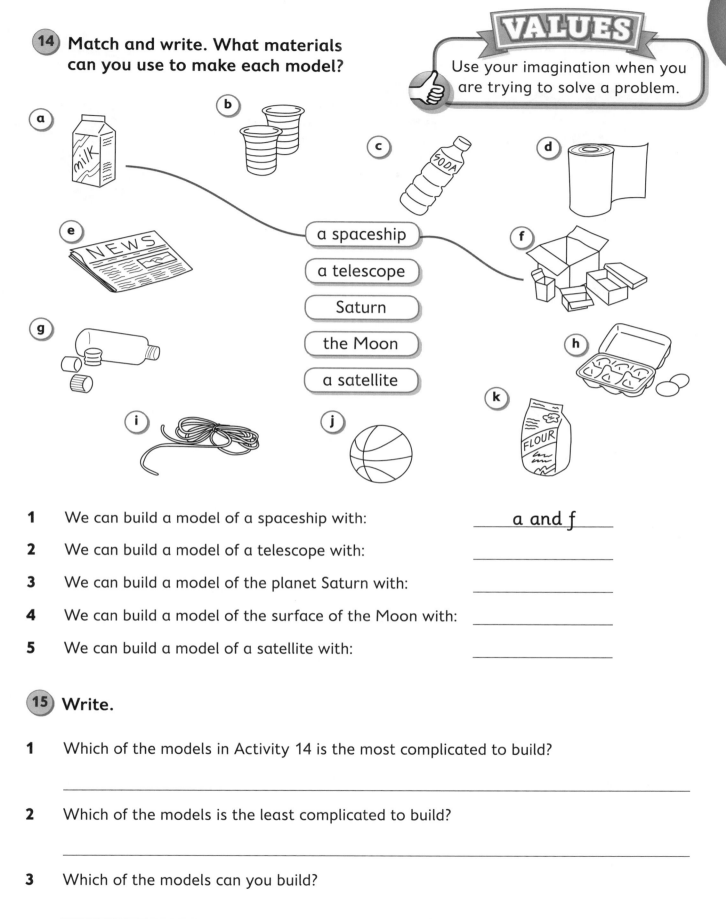

a spaceship

a telescope

Saturn

the Moon

a satellite

1 We can build a model of a spaceship with: _____a and f_____

2 We can build a model of a telescope with: _____

3 We can build a model of the planet Saturn with: _____

4 We can build a model of the surface of the Moon with: _____

5 We can build a model of a satellite with: _____

15 **Write.**

1 Which of the models in Activity 14 is the most complicated to build?

_____

2 Which of the models is the least complicated to build?

_____

3 Which of the models can you build?

_____

7

16   **Listen, check (✓), and number.**

a   The aliens thanked Jake.

b   Three days later, there was a postcard for Jake.

c   The aliens wanted to go to the fourth planet.

d   One alien said, "We're lost!"

17   **Write the second part of Connor's story. Use the questions to help you.**

1   What did Jake see in the field? How did Jake feel?

Jake saw _____.

_____

_____

_____

2   What did the aliens ask Jake? What did Jake say? Where did the aliens want to go?

An alien asked, "Where _____?"

_____

_____

_____

3   Did Jake dream about the aliens? What happened three days later? Was it a dream?

Jake went to bed and _____.

_____

_____

_____

18 Write.

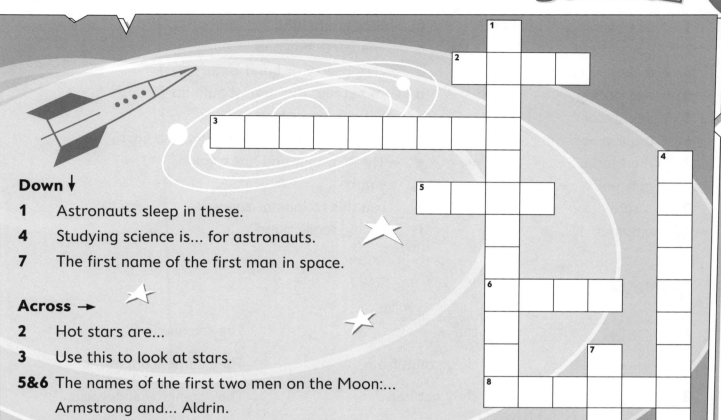

Down ↓

1 Astronauts sleep in these.

4 Studying science is... for astronauts.

7 The first name of the first man in space.

Across →

2 Hot stars are...

3 Use this to look at stars.

5&6 The names of the first two men on the Moon:...
Armstrong and... Aldrin.

8 Jupiter is closer to the Sun than this planet.

19 Can you remember the planets? Look at this phrase to help you.

Most **V**ery **E**xcellent **M**other **J**ust **S**ent **U**s **N**oodles

Mercury Venus Earth Mars Jupiter Saturn Uranus Neptune

20 Write a phrase to help you remember the planets.

M _____ V _____ E _____ M _____

J _____ S _____ U _____ N _____

21 Match.

1	intelligent	**a**	very interesting
2	amazing	**b**	The Earth has one.
3	complicated	**c**	very pretty or handsome
4	fascinating	**d**	something that you should do
5	important	**e**	difficult to understand
6	a telescope	**f**	not natural but goes around the Earth
7	the Moon	**g**	This is bright and has a tail.
8	gorgeous	**h**	smart
9	a satellite	**i**	use this to look at space
10	a comet	**j**	really, really good

22 Write.

1 _____ they?   They're aliens.

2 _____ they come from?   They came from Mars.

3 _____ they get here?   They came by spaceship.

4 _____ are you looking at the sky?   I think I saw a comet.

5 _____ that flashing light?   It's a satellite.

6 _____ you buy that telescope?   I bought it last week.

23 Unscramble and write questions. Then write your answers.

1 intelligent / whales / are / which / less / dogs / or

<u>Which are less intelligent, whales or dogs?</u>

My answer: _____

2 planet / which / most / the / interesting / is

_____

My answer: _____

3 science / more / is / or / English / which / difficult

_____

My answer: _____

24 **Listen and write.**

Which sneakers are the best for me?

I want to buy some new sneakers. There are three pairs ¹_____ I like.

The ²_____ pair is green with orange stripes. They look ³_____,

but they're the ⁴_____ expensive at $105! The ⁵_____ pair is

⁶_____ expensive. This pair costs $75. They look OK, but the first pair is

⁷_____ beautiful. The ⁸_____ pair is the ⁹_____

expensive at $20, but they aren't a good fit. My mom says price is the most

¹⁰_____. But I think how they look is the most important!

25 **Choose three things to buy. Write about them. Compare price, size, and how they look.**

_____

_____

_____

_____

_____

_____

_____

_____

_____

 Are you ready for Unit 8?

8 The environment

1 Write.

> paper   recycle   reuse   trash   turn off   use

1

recycle _____

2

pick up _____

3

_____ bottles

4

_____ plastic bags

5

_____ public transportation

6

_____ the lights

2 Write.

1 _____ people always reuse plastic bags.

2 _____ people sometimes reuse plastic bags.

3 _____ people usually reuse plastic bags.

4 _____ people never reuse plastic bags.

5 The total number of people was _____.

Do you reuse plastic bags?

3 Write.

1 I _____ reuse plastic bags.

2 I _____ use public transportation.

4   **Look at Tom's plans for next week. Listen and write.**

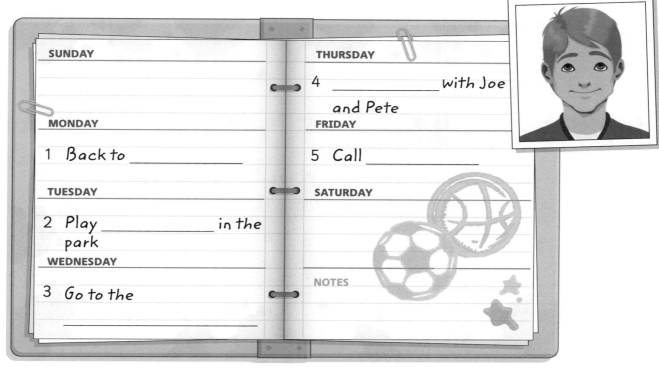

SUNDAY

MONDAY

1 Back to _____

TUESDAY

2 Play _____ in the park

WEDNESDAY

3 Go to the

_____

THURSDAY

4 _____ with Joe

and Pete

FRIDAY

5 Call _____

SATURDAY

NOTES

5 **Write questions about Tom. Then write the answers.**

Is Tom going to go back to school on Monday?

Yes, he is.

1 soccer / park / Tuesday _____

_____ _____

2 movie theater / Thursday _____

_____ _____

3 call / Joe / Friday _____

_____ _____

4 pizza / Thursday _____

_____ _____

6 **Write. What are you going to do next week?**

_____

7 **Match.**

1 What can you do to save trees?

2 What can you do to conserve energy?

3 What can you do to save resources?

4 What can you do to keep the planet clean?

a pick up trash

b recycle bottles

c recycle paper

d turn off the lights

8 **Write a green diary for next week. What can you do to save the Earth?**

SUNDAY

I'm going to _____

_____ .

MONDAY

TUESDAY

WEDNESDAY

THURSDAY

FRIDAY

SATURDAY

NOTES

9 **Write the words in the correct circle.**

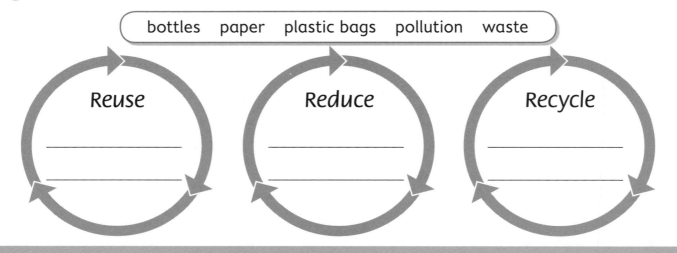

bottles   paper   plastic bags   pollution   waste

Reuse

Reduce

Recycle

10 **Listen and number.**

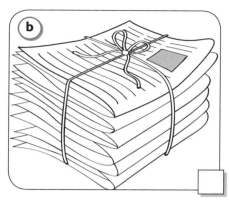

11 **Are you a good role model? Write about yourself.**

1 If you __recycle bottles_____ ,

you'll __save resources_____ .

2 If you _____ ,

you'll _____ .

3 If you _____ ,

you'll _____ .

4 If you _____ ,

you'll _____ .

5 If you _____ ,

you'll _____ .

6 If you _____ ,

you'll _____ .

12 **Check (✓).**

1 Who did AL give the chip to?

a b c

2 What did Dot and Zeb use to send a message to their people?

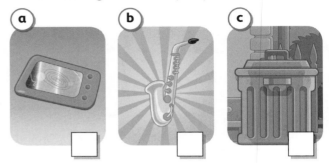

a b c

13 **Listen and number to match the people to what they said.**

1 "Did they go home in the end?"

2 "I have some news for you both."

3 "What! That's frightening!"

4 "They were aliens from Mars."

a b c d

12 **Circle or write your own answer.**

1 I think Bella is…
  a brilliant.
  b intelligent.
  c _____.

2 I think the THD is…
  a amazing.
  b complicated.
  c _____.

3 My favorite character is…
  a Matt.
  b Dot.
  c _____.

4 I think the story was…
  a brilliant.
  b fascinating.
  c _____.

15 Check (✓) the items you personally use daily. Then complete the diagram for yourself.

VALUES

Save our planet. Learn to save energy and keep the planet clean.

1 water ☐

2 electricity ☐

3 plastic cups ☐

4 batteries ☐

5 gas ☐

6 juice cartons ☐

7 milk cartons ☐

8 yogurt cartons ☐

9 writing paper ☐

10 soda cans ☐

11 wrapping paper ☐

12 plastic bottles ☐

13 food cans ☐

14 plastic bags ☐

15 paper bags ☐

16 cardboard boxes ☐

17 candy wrappers ☐

I'll reduce...

I'll recycle...

I'll reuse...

writing paper

16 Remind yourself what to do where. Complete the chart with items from Activity 15. Are there any differences?

	At school	At home
RECYCLE		
REDUCE		
REUSE		

17 **Write.**

bottles   buses   cleanest   going   plastic   tomorrow   trash

Hi Molly,

Your plans for ¹_____ sound fun! My class at school is going to have a Green Day. We're going to put all the ²_____ into different recycling bins, and then we're going to make Green Day posters for school. I'm going to pick up some trash, and others are going to bring paper, ³_____, and ⁴_____ bags. We're going to be the ⁵_____ school in our town! Then we're all ⁶_____ to walk or bike ride home – no cars or ⁷_____. I love bike riding, so I'm very happy! I'm going to like Green Day. Oh, and can I use your bike?

Thanks!

Niki

18 **Look at Activity 17 and write.**

1   What's special about tomorrow?   _____

2   What's Niki going to make?   _____

3   What does Niki want to borrow?   _____

4   Is Niki a "green" person?   _____

19 **Make lists.**

1   What are some of the causes of air pollution?

_____

_____

_____

2   What are some kinds of trash?

_____

_____

_____

20 **Find, circle, and correct each mistake.**

Venezuela

1 The highest waterfall in the world is Angel Falls in (Chile.) It's 979 meters high.

2 Australia is the smallest island and the smallest continent in the world.

3 The Atacama desert in Chile, South America, is probably the wettest place in the world.

4 The Nile in Africa is the longest river in the world, and you can see it in five countries.

5 Mount Fuji is a very famous lake in Japan, and it's the highest mountain in Japan, too.

21 **Circle.**

Our amazing world QUIZ

1 Niagara Falls in the U.S. is **?** than Angel Falls.

a higher

b 979 meters

c longer

d lower

2 Australia is the **?** continent in the world.

a biggest

b 2nd biggest

c 3rd biggest

d smallest

3 The biggest desert in the world is the **?** desert in North Africa.

a Gobi

b Atacama

c Sahara

d Arabian

4 The Amazon is the **?** longest river in the world.

a 1st

b 2nd

c 3rd

d 4th

22 **Match.**

1	conserve	**a**	a poison in the environment
2	reduce	**b**	save or keep
3	recycle	**c**	We use these to get food home from the store.
4	turn off	**d**	Buses and trains are two examples of this.
5	pollution	**e**	Light and heat are two examples of this.
6	public transportation	**f**	make less
7	trash	**g**	things that are used carelessly
8	plastic bags	**h**	change into material that we can reuse
9	waste	**i**	things we throw away
10	energy	**j**	opposite of turn on

23 **Circle.**

I'm going to help make my school greener. My friends and I are ¹(will / going to)
put recycling boxes in every classroom. Then we can ²(pick up / turn off) paper and
³(transportation / bottles) to recycle. My family is also going to help ⁴(reduce / save) the
planet at home. They're going to ⁵(use / turn off) the lights when they go outside, and
my mom is going to ⁶(use / reuse) public transportation to go to the supermarket. We
⁷(will / going to) all be greener!

24 **Unscramble and write. Then match.**

1 public / transportation / if / you / use

_____

a you'll save resources.

2 pick up / if / trash / you

_____

b you'll conserve energy.

3 you / recycle / if / paper

_____

c you'll reduce pollution.

4 the / off / lights / if / you / turn

_____

d you'll save trees.

5 recycle / if / bottles / you

_____

e you'll keep the planet clean.

8

25 **Listen and write.**

Tomorrow, I'm going to be home late from school ¹_____ I have band

practice. This week we are ²_____ at lunchtime and after school. We

are ³_____ play in a concert ⁴_____ week downtown.

⁵_____ going to play the clarinet, and my two best friends are going

to play the saxophone. ⁶_____ we play well, our teacher and parents

⁷_____ be very happy. My grandparents are coming, and after the concert

we ⁸_____ going to go out for ⁹_____. It should be a good

evening. I ¹⁰_____ practice now!

26 **Write a journal entry about your plans for the future.**

This weekend, I'm going to _____.

Then I'll _____.

Next week, _____.

_____

_____

_____

Next year, _____.

_____

_____

_____

_____

Goodbye

1 🎧 **Listen and circle T = True or F = False.**

53

a Matt's boss wanted to know where the new THD was.   T / F

b Matt and AL will go back to work.   T / F

c Zeb and Dot had a long journey home.   T / F

d They enjoyed their time on Earth.   T / F

e Bella didn't have to do her chores.   T / F

f She'll tell her friends about her adventures.   T / F

2 **Look at the pictures and answer the questions.**

1 Whose is this?   _____

2 What did they use it for?   _____

3 Who made this music?   _____

4 Why was it important?   _____

5 Whose is this?   _____

6 Where were they when they used it?   _____

3 **Answer the questions. Write *Yes, he/she/they/it did* or *No, he/she/they/it didn't*.**

1 Did the THD work after Bella looked at it?   _____

2 Was Bella good at helping Matt and AL?   _____

3 Was Matt angry at the end of the story?   _____

4 Was getting the new THD back important to AL?   _____

5 Did the Martins keep the new THD?   _____

6 Did Dot and Zeb go home to Mars?   _____

4 Circle.

1   What's Tom like? (Unit 1)

         He's smart and good at (singing / sports).

2   Who cooked a stew? (Unit 4)

         (Felipe / Flo) cooked a stew.

3   What will Felipe and Tom do first at the amusement park? (Unit 5)

         They will go on the water (slide / park).

4   What was Flo doing near the park in Unit 3?

         She was buying (chocolate / ice cream).

5   What were Flo and Tom doing on the hill in Unit 7?

         They were having a (party / campfire).

6   Where are Tom and Flo from? (Unit 1)

         They're from the United (States / Kingdom).

7   What does Hannah do to help clean up? (Unit 8)

         Hannah (doesn't help clean up / picks up the trash).

8   Where's Felipe from? (Unit 1)

         He's from (Spain / Mexico).

9   Where did Maria go in London? (Unit 5)

         She went to the (palace / aquarium) and the museum.

10   What's Maria not good at? (Unit 1)

         She's not good at (singing / surfing).

11   Who scared Maria outside the movie theater? (Unit 6)

         (Felipe / Flo) scared Maria outside the movie theater.

12   What was Tom doing in Unit 2?

         He was watching the (panthers / cheetahs).

13   What was Tom doing in Unit 8?

         Tom was recycling (bottles / paper).

14   How many steps are there in the castle in Unit 3?

         There are (450 / 540) steps in the castle.

5 Write.

My past

1 Last summer, I _____ .

2 Yesterday, I _____ by myself.

3 I've never _____ .

My present

4 I'm good at _____ .

5 I like _____ , but I don't like _____ .

6 I love _____ and _____ .

7 I can _____ , but I can't _____ .

8 There is a _____ my home.

9 I want to _____ .

10 I have to _____ .

My future

11 Tomorrow when I get up, first I _____ .

12 Then I _____ .

13 Next year, I _____ .

14 If I study hard at school, I _____ .

6 Draw three animals. Then write about them.

1 The _____ is taller than the _____ .

2 The _____ is the _____ .

3 The _____ .

4 The _____ .

7 Write.

how   what   when   where   which   who   why

1 _____ are you happy?

2 _____ is that bright light?

3 _____ is the most frightening?

4 _____ is your favorite movie star?

5 _____ do you live?

6 _____ do you get up?

7 _____ did you get here?

8 Make a poster about how to help the environment. Then write.

1 I'm going to _____.

2 What can you do to help?

I can _____.

3 If you _____, you'll _____.

Structures

Welcome

Does it look good?	Yes, **it does**. / No, **it doesn't**.
What **does it look like**?	**It looks** good.
	It looks like a cake.

Unit 1 Adventure camp

Flo is good at swimming.
I like hiking, but **I don't like** sailing.
I love fishing and camping.

I'm pitching the tent.
We're putting in the pegs.
I can pitch a tent, but **I can't read** a compass.

Unit 2 Wildlife park

How heavy **is it**?	**It's** 800 kilograms.
How tall **is it**?	**It's** 5 meters tall.
The giraffe **is taller than** the rhino.	
The giraffe **is the tallest**.	

Are otters **bigger than** seals?	Yes, **they are**. No, **they aren't**.
Were the giraffes **taller than** the trees?	Yes, **they were**. No, **they weren't**.
Which **is the heaviest**?	The hippo **is the heaviest**.

Unit 3 Where we live

How **do you get** to the school?
Go straight, then **turn** left at First Avenue.
It's **next to** the movie theater. It's **behind** the park. It's **at the end of** First Avenue.

I want to go to the park.	**He/She wants to go** to the park.
I have to go to the library.	**He/She has to go** to the library.

Unit 4 Good days, bad days

I cooked stew.	**He dropped** the plate.
She paddled very quickly.	**We fell** in the lake.

What happened?	**I didn't pass** my test **because I didn't study**.
	He didn't bring his juice **because he was late** for school.

Unit 5 Trips

What **did you do** yesterday?	**I went** to the aquarium.
Did you go to the aquarium?	Yes, **I did**. / No, **I didn't**.
Did you like the aquarium?	

What **will you do** at the amusement park?
First, **I'll ride** the Ferris wheel. Then **I'll go** on the bumper cars.

Unit 6 Arts

I saw the movie by **myself**.
You wrote it by **yourself**.
He made it by **himself**.
She didn't go to the movie by **herself**.
We didn't watch it by **ourselves**.
They didn't draw it by **themselves**.

Did you hear the cello?	Yes, **I did**. / No, **I didn't**.
Have you ever played the saxophone?	Yes, **I have**. / No, **I haven't**.
Have you ever been to a concert?	Yes, **I have**. / No, **I've never been** to a concert.

Unit 7 Space

Who are they?	They're astronauts.
When did they come?	They came last night.
Where did they come from?	They came from the Moon.
How did they get here?	They came by spaceship.
Why are you looking at the sky?	I saw a flashing light.
What's that flashing light?	It's a spaceship.

Which telescope **is more complicated**?	The big telescope **is more complicated than** the small telescope.
Which telescope **is the most complicated**?	The big telescope **is the most complicated**.
Which telescope **is less complicated**?	The small telescope **is less complicated than** the big telescope.
Which telescope **is the least complicated**?	The small telescope **is the least complicated**.

Unit 8 The environment

Are you going to recycle paper?	Yes, **I am**. No, **I'm not**. **I'm going to** recycle bottles.

What **can you do** to help?	**I can use** public transportation.
If you reuse plastic bags, **you'll reduce** waste.	